PUTIN'S
EVIL
EMPIRE

PUTIN'S EVIL EMPIRE

JOHN BURNHAM

In Memory of

John

CONTENTS

INTRODUCTION

WE GOT MARRIED IN MAY 1989. A few months later, in November, the Berlin wall came down. It was euphoric! Throughout Eastern Europe people were ecstatic with joy and happiness. After fifty years of communist KGB tyranny they could travel, speak freely, feel human again.

I had done business in East Berlin for many years before that, always passing though Checkpoint Charlie or through the S-Bahn connection at Friedrich Strasse. The piercing looks and suspicion in the eyes of the DDR border guards or the German shepherd dogs sniffing inside and under the car (lest you bring someone out of the country) were especially unpleasant and I never spent more than a few hours for the regular business meetings there.

I always stayed at the Intercontinental on the West side of the wall, near Kurfuerstendamm. Never wanted to spend any time on the East side as a tourist. It was too oppressive-everything grey, pavement stones from the Nazi era, the Albert Speer architecture with buildings blackened by soot and in need of paint and total renovation.

We visited East Berlin as tourists for the first time sometime in late November 1989. One of the first places we saw was the famous Fine Art museum where my wife, as usual, had to stop and ask the female guard a question pointing to one of the paintings. The guard, in a tight grey uniform, almost screamed at her to get on and not to stop – this is not a railroad station . . . obviously it was democracy's very early days in East Berlin.

Everywhere we went in Eastern Europe – Budapest, Sofia, Moscow or St. Petersburg – everything looked drab and grey after years of communist mismanagement and neglect.

Now, twenty-five years later things have changed, at least optically – the city centers of most cities are freshly painted, there are no Wartburg or Trabant cars anywhere (the DDR air polluting two-cycle cars made of plastic) and one can't even see the pride of Russia – the Moskvitch car anymore.

However, the main difference is that most East European countries now belong to the European Union (EU) as well as NATO. They have come back after fifty years of nightmares and, while many are still working on their various versions of democracy, they are all free and proud to be independent nations.

Their dreams came true after all.

We must thank two people for this miracle – Mikhail Gorbatchov and Ronald Reagan. It took a few more years for the Soviet Union to collapse, luckily without a civil war or armed conflict.

The former Soviet colonies (republics) quickly claimed sovereignty and established their own national hymns, flags and embassies around the world.

The Baltics joined the EU while the rest muddle through corruption and incompetence to this day, along with Russia, in a post-Soviet slow dance to nowhere.

First came the oligarchs and hyperinflation.

Then came the Commonwealth of Independent States.

And then came Mr. Putin.

Putin's Dream

THE EUROPEAN UNION was created to prevent future wars in Europe, and especially between two neighbors – France and Germany. Mr. Schuman's dream was that if nations work together as partners they won't have a reason to fight each other. Members of the future Union should join voluntarily and only after completing various Union rules and requirements as to judiciary, human rights, corruption, environment, etc. There is not one single member of the EU that has been forcefully dragged into the EU, quite the opposite, many of the aspiring members have had to wait in line for years until they are found eligible to join. Just ask Turkey how long she has been waiting in line.

Mr. Putin, too, had a dream. In his dream he saw a vast conglomerate of former Soviet colonies that must come together to create the Eurasian Union. This must start with a skirmish, a small invasion, a tiny annexation in order to test the waters for a further permanent integration.

This "Tough Love" Union is not offered to volunteers. In his dream Mr. Putin has already decided who will join. Nobody's excluded and there are no opt-outs. It is his way, not Mr. Schuman's. There is no need to fulfill any special requirements, corrupt and backward is a plus, and a despotic ruler is a bonus.

Needless to say Moscow will continue to be the capital of the new Union and everything will be just like the good old days of the Soviet Union:

The tomatoes are red, the cucumbers are fresh and it's all free, from the state. And Russia will be the greatest nation on earth.

Eurasian Union myth

IT IS REMARKABLE that no one has questioned the Eurasian Union myth. Nobody dared? Mr. Putin is always right (and he has a KGB stick too). How can any Union exist if it is forced onto its members? What kind of Union is one that includes nations that have different national goals and interests? And how can anyone imagine having a Union lead by an aggressor?

It will be interesting to see what happens in Belarus and Kazakhstan after their despotic leaders go. What type of leaders will replace them? Will the new generation of leaders want to continue as dependants of Russia (and be part of his Union) or make new friends? After all Belarus, is just next door to both Ukraine as well as Poland /the EU. The population there has already voiced displeasure with Mr. Lukashenko.

Twenty-five years after the end of the Cold War the world witnessed an armed invasion by a member of the UN Security Council, by a member of the OSCE and a guarantor of

Ukraine's territorial integrity. All East European nations are now terrified by a repeat of the grey KGB nightmare.

Mr. Putin's dream is their worst nightmare.

Just start with Georgia and Ukraine. Both have experienced first hand the effects of Mr. Putin's dream – both have lost territory and are only guessing when he'll invade again. They live in a nightmare.

But think of the nightmares the Baltics are having or even Kazakhstan.

All of these have large Russian populations, remnants of the Soviet empire.

At a whim Mr. Putin can invade in order to "liberate" these people, who incidentally elected not to return to Russia after all these years.

Just imagine Turkey, which in Ottoman times stretched all the way to Budapest, trying to "liberate" its nationals in the Balkans and beyond. Is she dreaming of Ottoman grandeur?

Or Greece, who ages ago settled all the port cities along the Mediterranean and Black seas? Simferopol may become Simferopolis and Sebastopol goes back to Sebastopolis. Is Greece dreaming of getting back Constantinopolis?

And what if Germany decided to get back Eastern Prussia, Kaliningrad?

Is Angela Merkel dreaming of this? I don't think so (some people in Kaliningrad may wish she did).

Dreams can be a tricky thing – they can get you in a lot of trouble. Fast.

There is no going back after Crimea's invasion. Mr. Putin and his KGB team are not the partners the EU and US thought they were. They are on a path of restoring the Soviet empire.

The Evil Empire.

Let me show you my guns
and then we can talk

PUTIN DIPLOMACY

PUTIN'S PR NIGHTMARE

MR. PUTIN'S DREAM was interrupted by a girl rock band "Pussy Riot," who demonstrated their desire to be free and feel human. Their aspirations are the same as any young people the world over – to be able to see, read, sing and say the things that are on their mind and be able to criticize a corrupt regime.

This band of young women in their 20s created a world-wide following after they performed a mock-concert at St. Basil's Cathedral in Red Square outside the Kremlin. They were immediately arrested, denounced as anti-Christs, fascists and Western agents. They were duly put in prison until Mr. Putin himself signed an amnesty they didn't ask for. He wanted to get rid of them before they became martyrs. They already are.

How can one possibly accuse a few young girls of being a threat to the state?

What kind of a state is it if it feels threatened by a few girls with guitars?

Must be a paranoiac and weak state, a KGB state.

It is very telling that the fear lies with Mr. Putin and the KGB around him.

These girls were stronger than him and stronger than the KGB bullies that dragged them to prison. And they are not giving up. Despite daily threats to their lives they are committed to perform and continue to work for freedom in Russia. They represent the majority of young people in Russia who are starved for freedom and who are disgusted with Putin's media manipulation.

These people are the only hope and future of the country. They are fearless also in their expression of support for Ukraine's pursuit of freedom.

While Putin's state TV and radio portray everyone protesting his rule as a fascist, people are already used to see through this as cheap propaganda. It is pitiful as it hasn't changed since the days of Stalin and his KGB detail.

Everyone who doesn't agree with Mr. Putin is a fascist- this always resonates with the population as they still have NAZI Germany in their collective psyche as enemy number one. What people don't realize is that the KGB uses the same methods as the NAZIS, the difference is only in the color of their shirts.

Putin's Ukraine Nightmare

Oⁿᵉ cᵃⁿⁿᵒᵗ ᵍᵉᵗ ᵐᵒʳᵉ ᵉᵛⁱˡ than Putin in his attempt to destroy the budding Ukrainian state. On its knees after decades of corruption and in urgent need of economic and political help Mr. Putin found it convenient to invade and annex Crimea just when Ukraine could not defend herself. In criminal law this would be considered premeditated murder. In international law it is simply a barbaric act of unprovoked aggression.

Putin's Crimea land grab is a mirror copy of Hitler's Sudeten annexation – the very fascist action that Putin uses as example of rightwing excess against young demonstrators at home. It is but a proof that the KGB and the NAZIS are just two sides of the same coin.

The Ukrainian demonstrators in the Maidan Square were also labeled fascists. There's daily evil propaganda on Russian TV trying to destroy the image of all Ukrainians as fascists. It is simply pathetic and not becoming a country like Russia. But what can they do – Mr. Putin is the wild card they've been dealt and they have to deal with it.

Both Pussy Riot as well as Ukrainian musicians are firmly of the opinion that Putin's days are over. That all he does is done because of his own insecurity, incompetence and his own psychology. Aggression is in his KGB DNA and he doesn't know better. It is up to the people to deal with him. And the rest of the world too.

Unfortunately he is surrounded by like-minded "professionals" who shoot first and ask questions later. They are not into diplomacy. Why use diplomacy when you can use a gun!

Putin's political life depends on Ukraine staying within Russia's claws. The fact that the people of Ukraine are trying to develop an independent country is a powerful psychological blow to the Russian ego. The feeling of rejection from the land Russia originally came from is huge and hard to swallow. Mr. Putin is afraid of being the man who "lost" Ukraine so he'll do everything possible to destabilize, blackmail, invade, annex Ukrainian territory in order to achieve his goal – a shaky government dependant on Russia for its economic and political survival.

A free and democratic Ukraine is his biggest nightmare.

Putin's Evil Medicine

In order to prevent future nightmares Mr. Putin's KGB doctors have developed a system of blackmail measures that may prevent his European(!) neighbors from considering joining the European Union.

1. Start with an embargo to cripple the EU aspiring state's economy

2. Raise the pressure by cutting off gas supplies

3. Triple the price of gas so that it will hurt more

4. Maintain a large army at the border to make it clear the unfortunate neighbor will be invaded unless giving up its aspirations and dreams of Europe

5. If the unfortunate state doesn't break up talks with the EU, organize a skirmish at the border, a small invasion or annexation.

6. All of these Evil Pills were given to Georgia, Moldova and Ukraine – three European states that aspire to

a future in Europe and want to get out of Moscow's backward pull. All three lost territory and there's no guarantee they won't lose even more if Dr. Putin believes is will kill their aspirations.

Ukraine, as the largest of the three neighbors has however seen the worst abuse and blackmail. Even while Mr. Putin's protégé Yanukovich was in power, Russia frequently blackmailed Ukraine with gas deliveries and/or prices, inordinate border delays for perishable goods, or "health" problems with foodstuffs entering Russia.

Mr. Putin's evil methods are his way of negotiating to obtain better prices, conditions or ruin the company that doesn't comply. Honoring a contract is not something Mr. Putin's state likes, and pity the party that signs an agreement with Russia.

Russia has embargoed the popular Georgian wines and mineral water as well as Moldovan wines, for "health reasons." Wine exports are crucial for the two countries' economies, and many vintners have gone bankrupt since the Russian market was cut off.

It is a nightmare for these countries who are not yet part of the global economy and have no access to world finance.

They are hostages of Dr. Evil and his team.

The Nightmares of Eastern Europe

Putin's Eurasian Union Dream is the nightmare of his neighbors. His land grabbing for "humanitarian" purposes has turned Russia into a reckless and irresponsible state in need of serious international actions for restraint.

No matter how much new territories Mr. Putin invades the stature of Russia has already been dramatically diminished. From a solid and responsible world power to a raging regional bully crying for attention. Mr. Putin's actions are now no different from North Korea's ruler. And like North Korea, Russia's population too will suffer the consequences of irresponsible adventures. Like Germany in the last century Russia too may end up with a smaller territory if she continues causing trouble.

Even worse, the dream of Eurasian Union may unravel before it even starts. Like the "Commonwealth of Independent States" (who were they anyway).

Like all empires (good or evil) Putin's too will come to pass.

Hitler's Reich was supposed to last for 1000 years, it didn't last fifteen.

But wait, maybe the Evil Empire doesn't exist—maybe it's only a dream?!

Unfortunately it does exist and it is a nightmare.

PUTIN'S UN CIRCUS

IN THE "GOOD OLD" SOVIET DAYS no one was allowed to travel in or out of the country. That includes not only Russia and the Soviet Union but the whole of Eastern Europe as well! Everyone was prisoner in their golden communist cages, fed a diet of propaganda, minimum staples and bland music. And vodka, lots of. So nobody could leave the country even if they wanted and many were imprisoned for even thinking about it. It is different today, everyone can leave the country (and millions have) if they wish and when they wish. So I wonder, why is it that the "vulnerable" Russian speakers in Crimea or Eastern Ukraine have to be defended by a whole army of thugs, in addition to the 40,000 Russian soldiers at the border? These people live in Ukraine, have lived and worked there for years, nobody forced them to stay and nobody's keeping them to stay. So why don't they leave and go to Russia if Ukraine is so bad? Russia, the aggressor, has the audacity to ask the UN Security Council to convene to discuss the wellbeing of people who do not like living in Ukraine!? If Russia is so concerned about these people why doesn't Mr. Putin offer them asylum? That's how other nations treat political or economic refugees. But so far no one has complained about persecution or torture.

And why does the UN Security Council agree to discuss this utter nonsense?

The aggressor wolf is concerned about the safety of the lambs?

The annexation of Crimea is only the beginning of Mr. Putin's New World "Order." Ukraine won't have a chance to establish a stable democracy unless the UN suspends Russia from the Security Council, that should be the minimum cost Russia should pay for its aggression.

'We're not pro-Russia militia – we're Pussy Riot'

Financial Times cartoon of April 17, 2014

PUTIN'S CHINA SYNDROME

T RUE, while evil rules in Russia, China is forging ahead and conquering the world with mass marketed products. Russia's loss is China's gain.

Top 5 manufacturing exports :

Made in China	Made in Russia
Toys	Vodka
Clothing	Vodka
Electronics	Vodka
Cars	Vodka
Bullet trains	Vodka

There must be a different approach behind China's economic miracle. Does China not care about security? What is the reason why its economy is so good and about to overtake the US as the biggest in the world? And all this happened during Mr. Putin's fifteen years in power! China's success is a thorn in Mr. Putin's side.

Are the Chinese smarter or just not as suspicious and reckless?

It takes self-confidence and restraint to act as a responsible power.

Russia lacks both.

ЛЕНИН–
ЖИЛ,
ЛЕНИН–
ЖИВ,
ЛЕНИН–
БУДЕТ ЖИТЬ!

Бл. МАЯКОВСКИЙ.

Return of the Evil Empire

To be correct, the Evil Empire (Reagan's term for the Soviet Union) never went away. The Soviet Union collapsed after 75 years of corrupt mismanagement but the KGB (the evil part), responsible for its internal security, stayed in place. In fact, while the communist party is no longer in power, it is now the KGB who rules the entire country.

Its main benefactor is Mr. Putin.

Internal security is important, in every country. What makes the KGB evil is the way it acts: suppressing freedom of expression, demonstrations and the media. Russian TV and radio are totally under Putin's control and anyone perceived as a threat to the state (i.e. Mr. Putin) will be turned into an enemy and treated accordingly. The evil ways of the KGB are numerous: persecution and prosecution for invented stories, tax fraud, bribery, murder, i.e. all the tools the KGB uses itself to keep its people in power.

Other than taking control of government from the communist party the KGB rule is no different from Soviet times, and the key words that were valid then are still valid today:

- Corruption

- Incompetence

- Mismanagement

- Waste

- Collapsing infrastructure

- High mortality rates

- Low fertility rates

- Poor nutrition

- Inefficient, unmotivated, unreliable work force

- Apathetic noncommittal public

A particularly ominous tool in KGB's box is the invention and distortion of facts in the media, a mass propaganda that keeps the population constantly paranoid, threatened by would-be conspirators or under attack from abroad.

Using the pretext of "protecting" Russian speakers abroad is a favorite tool that sends shivers everywhere in the former Soviet Union- from Ukraine in the West to Kazakhstan in the East, from the Baltics in the North to the Black Sea in the South.

Why use diplomacy when you can use a gun?

KGB RULE 666

Aversion to Diplomacy

The best diplomat is a Kalashnikov

KGB rule 378

It is clear that Mr. Putin has an aversion to diplomacy. Even while organizing a fantastic Winter Olympics extravaganza he'd been planning the invasion of Crimea without even thinking of what the international community may feel.

Total disregard for international law, total disregard for the agreements that Russia is party to. Total disregard of Russia's status as a member of the UN Security Council. Other than alienating the world community and Ukraine what can Russia possibly gain? What was Mr. Putin thinking? And if he's not thinking who thought of such preposterous action at the height of harvesting the Olympics goodwill! Who can be held responsible for squandering $53 Billion of goodwill!!?? Anyone?

Is anyone in Russia holding Mr. Putin responsible for anything? No? He's a hero? He knows best, he is God?! Sounds much like a personality cult, much like the guy in North Korea.

The evil team in the Kremlin have started publishing embarrassing private phone calls between US or EU diplomats regarding the crisis in Ukraine. However, Russian diplomats too are caught sometimes on tape.

Here below a leaked YouTube recording of two Russian diplomats possibly under the influence.

It is a 30th March 2014 discussion between two Russian ambassadors to Africa discussing the UN condemnation of the annexation of Crimea:

(1): It is simple from now on. I say to the morons at the EU that we've taken Crimea back and now follow Catalonia, Venice, Skotlandia (skot means animal in Russian) and Alaska. We'll rest after that.

(2): We'll rest at first.

(1): Then all these Latvians, Estonians and other Europeans as well as Romanians and Bulgarians we can kick all the way to where they belong.

(2): Even better, we should take over California, Miami and London where Russians are 95% of the population. Leave the Romanians and Bulgarians in the

EU together with the Baltic shits. I recently spoke to the EU ambassador who told me we should take back the Romanians and Bulgarians. But I replied: no way – you eat them with spoons.

Some diplomats these two! Must have been high on African vodka or stayed too long in the sun but the arrogance is telling.

They obviously feel emboldened by the annexation of Crimea and are dreaming of future glory and new conquests. The Soviet Union was so adamant about "helping" former African colonies and even Cuba. Now Russia wants to obtain new colonies herself. The collapse of the Soviet Union "never happened," this time it will be different.

A strange mindset for a country that keeps her own population in the dark ages. Crude, reckless and predatory 19th century behavior.

Exceptional Xenophobia

In the days leading to the Crimea annexation Mr. Putin set up a committee whose goal is to articulate Russia's Exceptionalism, her special (non-European!) civilization. The committee is to invalidate EU principles of tolerance and multicultural heritage and emphasize Russia's own civilization developments.

The result would be to promote Russian values and reject any foreign and minority influences.

As noted it took 75 years for the Soviet Union to implode due to exceptional corruption and mismanagement.

All these years the population were kept in the dark about the economy and lived in fear of attacks from imaginary foreign powers, fifth columns and CIA agents. Mr. Putin has chosen the timing of his new initiative wisely, in the midst of worldwide outrage about his invasion. Let us focus on the traitors amidst us rather than the brave Ukrainians that are trying to build a free state! Let us focus on the foreign agents rather than the failing economy.

God help those foreigners or minorities who happen to live in Russia, invest in Russia or own a business there.

Mr. Putin has plans for you: pack up and go! But isn't this what the NAZIS did in Germany? Isn't this pure and evil xenophobia from the 1930s?

Beware of the enemy!

"Fifth column fascist traitors" marching in support of Pussy Riot.

Following the Crimea annexation Mr. Putin's popularity went up to 80%. Since he manipulates the media it is difficult to prove whether this is true. But if true why does he need to shower the public with alerts of a "fifth column" and "traitors everywhere." What is he afraid of? There are websites inviting people to point out traitors (i.e. critics of the annexation). Stalin's xenophobic times are back. The impression that the country is "under attack" diverts the attention from failures of the economy and lets the KGB get away with 1930s propaganda.

Is Mr. Putin really interested in the plight of his compatriots abroad or is he simply using these tactics to keep his neighbors docile? And why would he be concerned only about Russian speakers? Isn't it normal and human to be concerned about the wellbeing of all? How about the minorities in Russia proper, making up almost 20% of the population without language rights, many working in slave-like conditions and taking up the worst jobs so they can send money to their families in the former republics?

These modern day slaves are being abused daily on Russia's streets by NAZI-inspired skinhead gangs but are not given any protection by the Russian state. Why? They speak Russian too! Xenophobia is a disease in a society cut off from the world via KGB propaganda that sees no future, no hope and vents its frustration on the very people that sustain it for a miserable pay.

It is clear that "concern" about Russians abroad is just a smokescreen that the KGB uses to justify invasions and annexations of foreign territory just like Hitler did eight decades ago! The smokescreen is the necessary diversion so that nobody questions the failing economy and the state of things at home. Nobody should question Mr. Putin's tactics as the state is "under threat" and Mr. Putin is doing all he can to protect it.

From another collapse?

The evil is applied everywhere:

- Russian citizens (lack of basic freedoms and control of media)

- Minorities in Russia (xenophobia)

- Foreigners in Russia (xenophobia)

- Russia's Neighbors (economic blackmail)

- Eastern Europe (economic blackmail)

- Western Europe (economic blackmail)

The evil in the Evil Empire is the force that prevents new ideas, dissent and innovation as well as the motivation to prosper. The evil defends the status quo at any cost, even at the cost of another economic collapse. It is a very narrow-minded self-preservation strategy that will eventually lead to its own demise. The question is not if but when.

Adolf's Dream

THERE ARE ONLY TWO EXAMPLES of evil empires in the previous century: Nazi Germany and the Soviet Union.

The first one was destroyed from the outside.

The second collapsed on its own.

Interestingly, in both cases they were equally evil at home and abroad and were ruled by ruthless and reckless individuals who always "knew better" than the people around them.

Hitler had a dream of conquering all of Europe and expanding East.

Signing a non-aggression treaty with Stalin may have created a Eurasian Union of sorts but then he changed his mind and attacked his partner. It was not enough that he already owned most of Europe,

He had to have access to Eurasian labor. Luckily, he didn't succeed.

But *the lesson is important for those who want to learn from history.*

The problem with aggressors is that they never know when to stop – they are serial repeaters, invasions and annexations are in their DNA. They are addicts. There is no medical treatment for such personalities. It all ends sadly in the end.

Hitler's dream became a nightmare for a whole continent, and lasted another fifty years for its Eastern part after the end of the war. Like a raging bully – a monster.

Instead of gaining territory Germany lost almost one-third of its own.

And millions perished.

And it all started with a small invasion, a tiny annexation of the Sudetenland. Did anyone care? Were any sanctions applied or costs imposed? Wasn't WWI bad enough so another war had to start.

Didn't Hitler learn a lesson after WWI?

Obviously not.

Josef's Dream

Nobody knows whether Stalin ever had a dream, he never slept for fear of assassination. But whatever he did he did well. He chased Hitler's armies all the way to Berlin and hoisted the red flag atop the Reichstag. He then put a red line through Germany and colonized all Eastern European countries for the next fifty years. In addition he managed to exterminate almost twenty million of his own people: Russians, Ukrainians, minorities. Young, old and sick, rich or poor –they were all under suspicion for subversive activities. State security above all!

Yes, Josef did well in real estate – half of Europe and he cleaned Russia of minorities too – let them go East and stay there! Tatars from Crimea, Circassians from Sochi, Germans from the Volga – get out of your ancestral lands and move to Asia. Or else!

So who was more evil – Stalin or Hitler?

If Adolf was full of megalomania Josef was full of paranoia. Both were aggressors and murdered millions. The whole world sided with Stalin to defeat Hitler. And he used this goodwill to perpetuate his evil empire.

I would argue that, psychologically, Stalin's evil is by far longer lasting.

In fact it lasts to this day both in Eastern Europe as well as in the countries of the former Soviet Union. Stalin's evil and paranoiac rule via the KGB extinguished any initiative, robbed people of their own dreams and imagination. Lack of motivation is a plague that continues throughout many Eastern countries to this day.

This is especially visible in Russia and the former Soviet Union republics. The labor force is apathetic, reckless and, to this day, expects someone else to tell them what to do on a daily basis. Their psyche is scarred for life – after two generations of communist rule in Eastern Europe and three generations for the former Soviet lands. Hitler's war killed people but didn't rob their fantasies.

Entrepreneurship, a necessary combination of initiative, imagination and the will to succeed is a very scarce commodity in these countries, thanks to comrade Stalin and his KGB. It needs to be encouraged by any means to help these countries succeed.

Entrepreneurs have no chance in Putin's Russia (or his Eurasian Union).

For entrepreneurs to thrive Mr. Putin needs to set the whole society free: from TV and press to free speech and expression. Will the KGB allow that?

Doubtful. The KGB's focus is on security and on perpetuation of the state of fear in society, not on economic welfare. They protect the empire.

Mr. Putin regrets the loss of real estate from the Soviet collapse. Both in his home Reich as well as Eastern Europe. He now needs a visa to travel there and is only a tourist. He yearns for the old days when Russia owned these lands. He can't let go of the past. And he doesn't want to learn a lesson from history.

2017

Octstober 2017 will be the centenary of the 1917 October revolution.

Will Lenin remain in his mausoleum? Will anything change over the next few years? Doubtful, if Mr. Putin is still in power. It is more likely that he will use this anniversary to celebrate his dream of Eurasian Union, possibly with yet another annexation. Or will he wait for the 2018 Olympics?

Whose guns will start the celebrations in 2017? The cruiser Aurora in St. Petersburg or Sebastopol's fleet? Conventional guns or a nuclear submarine? Who will be targeted? Who will be appointed enemy No.1 for the occasion? Surely it cannot be corruption and incompetence at home!

Yes, let's celebrate the Eurasian Union in style, like the Sochi Olympics.

Who cares about infrastructure and diversifying the economy. As long as there's oil and gas (and vodka) Russia will be just fine.

But wait, what if the Russian people get emboldened by Ukraine's example and rise up and another revolution ensues? They have nothing to celebrate, they have nothing to celebrate with!

They've had enough of tough rule, tough guys and tough language.

Enough of suspicions, invasions, liberations and annexations.

Russia needs friends but who will want to be friends with an aggressor?

Especially her neighbors-the most natural friends of any country.

And what if Belarus gets rid of Yanukovich's twin Lukashenko?

What if Belarus quits the Union and goes her own way like Ukraine?

That wouldn't be a cause for celebration, of course. It will ruin Mr. Putin's dream for a Union of the basket cases. But he can use the occasion to annex Belarus!

When will the Russian people start asking about the missing oil and gas billions. Gold and metals too? What good is a car if you can't get to your house because of the endless dirt roads?

And how about China ? How is it they made it in fifteen years of Putin rule and we're still stuck in the mud?

LESSONS FOR MR. PUTIN

I T DOESN'T LOOK LIKE Mr. Putin is interested in history. If he is it is certainly only selectively – he wants to reverse the "greatest geopolitical catastrophe" of the last century (the collapse of the Soviet Union), and create a new Eurasian Union, by force if necessary. Union of the unwilling?

By annexing Crimea Mr. Putin has already taken the initial step on the path that Hitler took in the Sudeten. So that lesson was not learned.

But then why not learn the lesson of the collapse of the Soviet Union?

The country was not attacked by outsiders. There was no revolution.

The money simply ran out. It ran out because the economy didn't work and so much was wasted on the military. The economy didn't work, because of corrupt and incompetent management. And also because the workforce didn't work: "we pretend to work and they pretend to pay us" went the slogan. So how is a nation to succeed if nobody works? Is this a good lesson to learn? And how about money spent on invasions – where does it come from?

Meanwhile Germany, the defeated nation, rose from the ashes to become the world's largest exporter! Whatever happened to victorious Russia?

One must study the reasons and lessons for this collapse because it was the *greatest peacetime economic collapse*. One must study it carefully before contemplating another union. And one must learn to manage his own country first before forcing others into union. In any case the union should be voluntary, people must aspire to join and not be punished with membership.

The main lesson Mr. Putin should take from the Maidan square is the *toppling of the statue of Lenin*.

Lenin was the father of the October revolution, communism and the Soviet Union, and the misery it brought throughout Eastern Europe. Most of the former Soviet republics tore down their Lenin statues long ago, and Ukraine's act is just another reminder: communism didn't work, can't work and won't work. And as long as Russia keeps Lenin in a mausoleum the system of corruption will self-perpetuate and Russia will forever remain a hopeless emerging market. Russia badly needs a new role model!

AFTERMATH

Dealing with Evil

THE GOOD NEWS is that the memories of dealing with the Soviet Union are still fresh – containment, not appeasement.

The bad news is that containment may not be enough to deal with Mr. Putin.

The Soviet Union lasted for 75 years before it collapsed. Is the world going to wait 75 years for another collapse? Just think of Russia's population, shrinking fast and in desperate need of freedom.

Mr. Putin has shown that he has no use for diplomacy, so why continue negotiating? Do we negotiate with kidnappers and blackmailers?

The US and Europe overestimate and flatter Russia's role for "helping" the negotiations with Iran and Syria. What good is the signature of a pariah state on a document that is supposed to guarantee a certain future behavior between countries? Russia has proven that she cannot be a reliable partner in any agreement so why include her in such sensitive talks? At least limit the signatures to exclude Russia.

Russia's signature is not worth the paper it's written on.

For her aggression and annexation of Crimea, Russia should be suspended from the UN Security Council as well as the OSCE and other multilateral bodies. Mr. Putin should be treated as a pariah. Treat his whole circle as pariahs.

Limit Foreign Direct Investment into Russia and reduce purchases of Russian oil, gas or other products to reduce Russia's revenues.

Help Ukraine's economy and management thereof. Help her get rid of corruption. Make Ukraine a model former Soviet republic.

That would be the best cure for Mr. Putin's addiction.

As Ukraine prospers, Belarus may follow, then Kazakhstan, and that will be the end of Mr. Putin's dream of an Eurasian Union.

He'll realize his dream was a nightmare.

УКРАЇНА

(11) **65662**

Dear Sir,
Your Acquisition of Crimea

It is now several weeks since your esteemed professionals took over our land in the Crimea. It looks like the Russian population really liked this heroic act and your popularity has grown. No doubt you will want to settle this dispute amicably so that you can be assured a peaceful enjoyment of this magnificent property.

We ask you to settle the following costs associated with your acquisition:

Real estate Value: Euro 50billion
+ Premium for Historic Provenance: Euro 5 billion
+ Premium for Naval base: Euro 200 million
+ Premium for airport and other military facilities: Euro 200million
+ Penalty for trespassing: Euro 50million
+ Penalty for loss of income from rent at Naval base: Euro 250 million
+ Cost for repatriation of Ukrainians: Euro 250 million
+ Miscellaneous: Euro 50 million

Total : Euro 56 billion

We thank you for your attention and look forward to a quick and amicable settlement.

Regards,

We the people
Maidan
Kiev
Republic of Ukraine

www.ingramcontent.com/pod-product-compliance
Lightning Source LLC
Chambersburg PA
CBHW051128290526
45796CB00001B/2